BEWARE OF THE HIPPO

AND OTHER BEASTS ON THE RIVER OF LIFE

ROD WECKWORTH
WITH ALEX VON ALLMEN

Forward

As a physician I took a pledge that was a modern version of the ancient Hippocratic Oath. In summary, it requires us to "First, do no harm." Throughout life, we are consistently challenged. Frequently, our response to these challenges is far from ideal, and puts ourselves and others at risk of harm. Much of my life has been dedicated to helping my patients avoid harm in their journey towards health. This book provides great insights into how to avoid that harm.

Life's challenges, and our response to them, are often powerful in their ability to mold us. In his book, *Beware of Hippos and Other Beasts on the River of Life*, author, patient, and friend Rod Weckworth creatively describes the multiple variations of life's trails that are brilliantly embodied by the wild beasts we know. These powerful and vivid comparisons make his lessons and wisdom easy to digest and remember. As a cancer and reconstructive surgeon, I have seen many of my patients confront these challenges and beasts in their different forms. The strength and grace with which my patients navigate these hurdles are powerful reminders of the courage and capacity of the human spirit. With the wisdom on these pages, we can adapt to challenges, avoid harm, and live to our full potential.

I know you will love this book and the creative way Rod Weckworth weaves inspiration and promise into his text. May we all learn from his book to better navigate the hippos and other beasts on the river of life.

D. Gregory Farwell, MD FACS
Professor and Chair of Otorhinolaryngology-Head and Neck Surgery
University of Pennsylvania

Preface

As I reflect upon my life, I have learned many lessons about what it takes to be a leader. I have written this book to help others become better leaders and navigate both their personal and professional lives.

As we grow older our faces become our biographies.

- If you want happiness for an hour…take a nap.
- If you want happiness for a day…go fishing.
- If you want happiness for a year…inherit a fortune.
- If you want happiness for a lifetime…help others.

You can travel over the whole world in search of what you need, and then return home to find it. It was probably always there!

"Watch your character, for it becomes your destiny." - Lao Tzu

Ronald Reagan once said "The greatest leader is not necessarily the one who does the greatest things. **He is the one that gets the people to do the greatest things**."

Leadership is NOT about managing tasks. It is about inspiring others to be better than they thought they could be. It is about providing opportunities and reasonable resources for your team members to do things they only previously imagined. Leadership is about setting the vision and guiding the team in their ability to fulfill the vision.

What if You Lived Life Backwards? (Tomb to womb)

- You start out dead and get that out of the way.
- Then you wake up in a retirement home feeling better every day.
- You get kicked out for being too healthy.
- Go collect your pension.
- You start work, you receive a gold watch, and party on your first day.
- You work for 40 years until you're young enough to enjoy your retirement. You party and act out your dreams. Then you are ready for high school.
- Attend elementary school.
- You become a kid! You play and you have no responsibilities.
- You become a baby until you are born. Then you spend your last 9 months floating in luxurious spa-like conditions with central heating and room service on tap with larger quarters every day.
- Then BOOM, it all starts from scratch!

Perhaps we have reached the pinnacle of success. We can rise in the morning and go to bed at night, and in between, let's do whatever we want to do.

Introduction

South African farmer Marius Els was found dead in a river, mauled to death by his pet hippo. He had referred to the hippo as being "like a son to me." He had been bitten repeatedly by the animal.

Hippos are thought to be the most dangerous mammals in Africa. Their mammoth jaws are extremely strong, and their teeth weigh an average of 6.5 pounds each and can grow up to 1.2 feet long. Astonishingly, these gigantic animals can also run up to 30 miles per hour, so charging opponents is easy. Never try to outrun a hippo unless you have a turbo charger.

Even predators as fierce as lions have reasons to be cautious around these massive beasts. Lions are afraid of adult hippos but have been observed attacking baby hippos. On a rare occasion a lion will attack an old, weak, or frail adult hippo.

"Forewarned, forearmed; to be prepared is half the victory." wrote Miguel de Cervantes. The future belongs to those that best prepare for it. The key insights illustrated in this book are the result of 55 years of survival in the business world as an electrical and engineering contractor. There are several strategies that I have found vital for navigating through the river of life:

- Identify the problems ahead.
- Provide a clear actionable plan of navigation including defining your finish line…if you want to cross it.
- Solve the issues in a timely manner.
- Advance to the next level.
- Repeat-Repeat-Repeat. Use caution and every now and then look back and make sure that the calvary is still behind you.

Along the way, I have learned of these metaphorical threats on our journey through life:

- The Anacondas want to squeeze us to death.
- The Hippos don't want us in their territory.
- The Piranhas want to bite us along the way.

  If we survive the first three…
- Then, the Crocodiles want to eat us for dinner!

This book is a cautionary road map on how to survive the journey and advance through the river of life by adapting to the ways of nature and the animal-like creatures we encounter along the way.

Seek higher ground when crossing a swamp full of crocodiles.

Table of Contents

Chapter 1: Eagle

"Where there is no vision, the people perish."
- Proverbs 29:18a

In terms of knowing the choices we make…it is knowledge that we need to gain…But in terms of principles…let wisdom have its reigns - then the right decision can be made.

Chapter 1: Eagle - The Vision

Eagles are natural born leaders. They are raptors with keen vision and high intellect who soar above scanning the Earth below. These "warbirds" are sharply focused on their objectives and like fighter pilots, are not afraid to engage in conflict, debate, and battle. No wonder an "eagle" landed on the moon.

Alexander the Great - the Gordian Knot

As the story goes, in 333 B.C. Alexander marched his army into Gordium in modern day Turkey. Upon arriving in the city, he encountered "several knots all so tightly entangled that it was impossible to see how they were fastened." An oracle had declared that any man who could unravel its elaborate knots was destined to become ruler of all of Asia.

Alexander wanted to untie the Gordian knot. After wrestling with it for a time and finding no success, he stepped back from the mass of gnarled ropes and proclaimed, "It makes no difference how they are loosened." He then drew his sword and sliced the knot in half with a single stroke.

The moral of the story is that once you remove the barriers in life then you enable action. ***Be bold and confident and find a creative way to handle what seems like an insurmountable problem.*** *Removing the barriers in life will often enable us to take the shortest route to success.*

Thinking Outside the Box

Are you able to connect all nine dots without lifting your pencil from the paper?

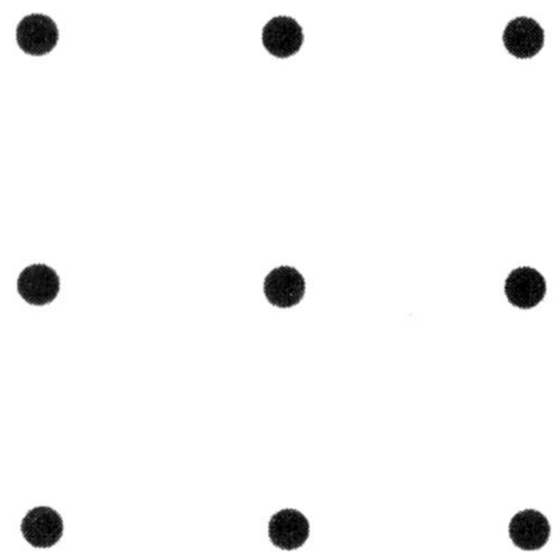

You can solve this problem with just 4 lines if you go outside the 9-dot box limitation created by your mind. You need to tap into your inner eagle...or think like Alexander the Great.

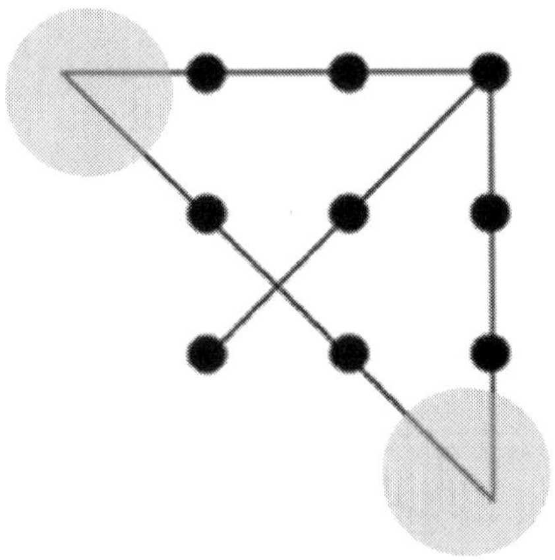

It's those hidden boundaries that hinder our journey toward success.

What can we learn from the Eagle?

- Eagles Have Vision – They view challenges and opportunities from a 10,000-foot perspective.
- Eagles are focused. They are analytical yet decisive.
- Eagles never fly in flocks! Never simply go with the crowd. Be with others who are at your level or above to help you grow. Don't expect others to share your vision. Don't waste time with negative people who want to crush your dreams.
- Eagles are fearless and never surrender, never quit, and they are bold and dominant.
- Uses the wind to lift us to a higher level. Welcome the storms and use the wind to fly up to a higher elevation above the turmoil to become stronger.
- The eagle prepares the nest carefully in which to raise their young. Then teaches the young eagle to fly by trial and error.
- "May you soar on eagle wings, high above the madness of the world." Jonathan Lockwood Huie
- "In order to fly, you have to let go of the world you're hanging onto." - Kurek Ashley
- Keep current with learning and keen observation.
- Accept the storms of life. Use them to strengthen our position. Embrace knowing that if we persevere, we will be stronger.
- Never become complacent and satisfied in life with the old way of doing things. Explore ways to think differently or to see things from a new perspective.
- Look for challenges ahead and get out of the nest.

Vision Keeps Us Focused and Motivated

Besides providing perspective for solving problems, vision becomes the foundation for our journeys. It is a mental picture of what the future can hold. It is the thing inside of us that guides us. It creates a desire to grow and improve. Vision embodies our hopes, dreams, and ideals. It gives us a sense of purpose. Vision keeps us motivated, provides focus and allows us to move through obstacles. Helmuth von Moltke the Elder once wrote, "No plan survives first contact with the enemy." So, the secret to winning the war is to always be planning.

Vision is Strategic.

Chinese military general Sun Tzu in "The Art of War" wrote "Strategy is about winning before the battle is ever fought" and "Tactics without strategy is the noise before defeat. The greatest victory is that which requires no battle." Use your intelligence as opposed to your brawn to win. You can enter conflict prepared for anything if you have a sense of your strengths and abilities. Planning and preparation are key, especially in terms of knowing your opponent. Know their strengths and vulnerabilities to preemptively strike. Always have a contingency plan. If you can win a battle with integrity as opposed to winning by obliteration of the opponent, people will have greater respect for you.

Application

Most of us get caught up in what Charles Hummel describes as the "tyranny of the urgent." Sometimes we need to step back from our busy lives and view a problem from another perspective. We need to stop and take a deep breath. Refocus and ask ourselves whether there are different paths to reaching our goals. We may want to question whether our goals still make sense.

A positioning map is a great example of the ten-thousand-foot view and is a great way to uncover opportunities in business. When Apple was developing a new phone, they segmented the portable phone market into "smart versus not so smart" and "hard versus easy to use". The iPhone seemed to fit in the "smart and easy to use" area. ***Opportunities are where your competitors are not.***

Apple iPhone Launch

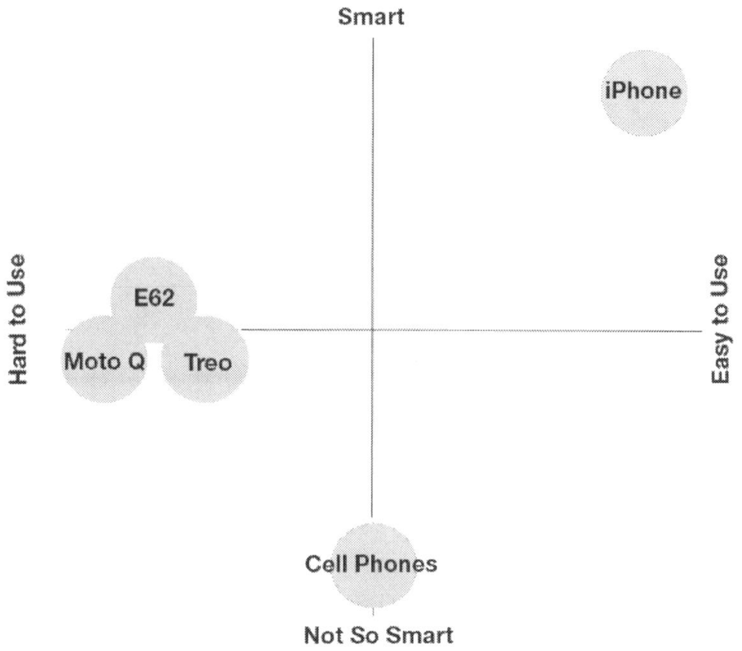

In the late sixties people were not drinking 7-Up. Most people considered it primarily a mixer or a tonic for an upset stomach. Company executives tasked an advertising agency to rebrand their soda to compete with established brands like Coke and Pepsi. JWT created a campaign to frame 7-Up as the "Uncola". Instead of focusing on similarities it shared with competitors, 7-Up was showcased as being distinctly different in look and taste. They attracted customers by stating what they were not. Even today when you think Uncola you think of 7-Up. That is effective 50-year-old advertising!

Thoughts for Reflection

- " If you pick the right people and give them the opportunity to spread their wings...and put compensation and rewards as a carrier behind it...you almost don't have to manage them." - Jack Welch
- "A fool with a plan is better than a genius with no plan" - T. Boone Pickens
- "By failing to prepare, you are preparing to fail." - Benjamin Franklin
- "Act like the person you want to become." - Ruben Chavez
- "If you don't know where you are going, any road can take you there." - Lewis Carroll
- "In the absence of clearly defined goals, we become strangely loyal to performing daily trivia until ultimately, we become enslaved by it." - Novelist Robert Heinlein
- "If you know the enemy and know yourself, you need not fear the result of a hundred battles." - Sun Tzu
- "Choose your own direction-rather than climb on the bandwagon." - Peter F. Drucker
- "Leaders must encourage their organizations to dance to forms of music yet to be heard." - Warren G. Bennis
- "Ability is nothing without opportunity." - Napoleon Bonaparte

- “Vision is the art of seeing what is invisible to others.” - Jonathan Swift
- “Leadership is the capacity to translate vision into reality.”- Warren Bennis
- “I am not afraid of an army of lions led by a sheep; I am afraid of an army of sheep led by a lion.” - Alexander the Great
- “A leader is best when people barely know he exists, when his work is done, his aim fulfilled, they will say: we did it ourselves.” - Lao Tzu
- “A leader is one who knows the way, goes the way, and shows the way.” - John Maxwell
- “Innovation distinguishes between a leader and a follower.” - Steve Jobs
- “It always seems impossible until it's done.”- Nelson Mandela
- “Vision without action is merely a dream. Action without vision just passes the time. Vision with action can change the world.” - Joel A. Barker

Chapter 2: Anaconda

``When you squeeze an orange, orange juice comes out - because that's what's inside. When you are squeezed, what comes out is what's inside." - Wayne W. Dyer

Chapter 2: Anaconda - The Squeeze

Pound for pound, the largest snake species in the world is the green anaconda. The biggest one on record was 29 feet long and weighed in at 550 pounds. They are primarily aquatic, nocturnal and live in South America.

When prey crosses their path, the anaconda first strikes without eating or swallowing it. The snake coils around the prey with its body until it has suffocated it. Both their jaws and their skin can expand, allowing them to swallow meals of a great size. Their breath has a terrible stench.

Competition is the Squeeze

Competition for limited time, exerts energy and resources as a squeeze on us. Most of us have both obligations and the things we desire in life. There are other applicants for that school, job, mate, or house we want. And don't forget there are bills and taxes to pay. Sometimes our eyes are bigger than our stomachs and our stress is self-imposed. We need to ask what brings us real joy.

Dealing effectively with the competition for time and energy is about having the discipline to figure out what is most important to you. When you know what you really want you can better focus your resources. Acting quickly and decisively can make a difference.

Meeting Helena

It was a summer afternoon; I was eighteen and my friend and I were driving a car down Broadway. We saw two girls walking and pulled over to talk to them. One of the girls gave me her name "Helena Nelson" but no phone number. The next day I discovered that there were over 80 Nelsons in the phonebook. So, I started calling each number asking, "Is there a Helena Nelson at this number?" Somewhere around the middle of the list, Helena's father answered thinking that I was asking for his wife who was also named "Helena". I got permission to come over. The sixteen-year-old daughter Helena was still out babysitting so I had a nice chat with her father.

When Helena arrived home she uttered, "What are you doing here?" Her father intervened and said, "Rod seems like a nice young man. He would like to take you for a drive. It is okay with me". That was our first date, and we were married three months later.

Today we have been married for over 58 years and have three children, grandchildren, and even great grandchildren. Finding a life partner has made all the difference in my life and goals. Both of us as teenagers experienced difficult home lives. We were both being squeezed, and marriage offered us an opportunity to escape the pressure. Avoiding the squeeze enabled Helena and I to create a wonderful life and business together instead of just making a living.

Learning from the Anaconda

I've learned much from a lifetime of "squeeze" experiences. Here are some big ones:

- We all make mistakes, but the only real mistake is not learning from them.

- It's important to get a firm grasp of reality. Discern what is true and what is false.

- Embrace the squeezes that we come across daily. They are how we learn and build character.

A person knocked down by another can get up again, but a person squeezed to the limits and by conformity stays down for good.

With the squeeze around us from all directions- we learn that understanding human needs is half the job of meeting them.

Getting past the squeeze means we need to develop to the point of our limitations and then!!...Break those limitations...leaving the old baggage outside the front door.

Applications

My career has been in electrical contracting and engineering. Most contractors entering trades believe that if they provide a good service at a reasonable price, they will be fine. **But the anaconda in the form of competition has other plans.** Unfortunately, most contractors struggle because they don't understand what their customers really want. This miscommunication leads to being squeezed...sometimes out of business.

I was fortunate enough to learn early that I could get an edge by really listening to customers, discovering their needs, and building trusting relationships. Thus, avoiding the squeeze.

We were always looking for ways to create value for our customers. Today we use a survey that helps us rate our customers' needs in 25 areas including quality, expediency, safety, price and more. I discovered that most of our customers valued quality first, then expediency. Then they wanted the project completed at or below budget. Pricing does matter but it's usually further down on the list.

I recommend learning to recognize all aspects of value you can create for your customers. That might include peace of mind for them to meet their deadlines. If you believe that price is the only differentiator, you might want to rethink that position.

Trust is very important, and it takes time to build. In our business, trust means being competent to deliver in a timely manner, being honest in all dealings, and having clients and team members' best interests at heart.

A long-term client came to me needing the electrical work done on a large wine making facility. It was a multimillion-dollar job and I told him that I didn't feel I had the resources to complete the assignment. He surprised me by structuring the terms and payments in a way that would allow us to deliver a quality service. We completed the project on time and the 3 million square foot facility became a reality.

Companies and government agencies will publish a request for proposal (RFP) to solicit proposals from qualified contractors. This is called competitive bidding. This process maintains a competitive marketplace, as contractors must submit their best propositions and compete for specific projects. A second-place bid fails to win the contract.

Contract bids, like horse races, are often won by a nose. "Sham" is regarded as one of the fastest racehorses of all time, but you probably haven't heard of him. He spent his career chasing Triple Crown winner Secretariat, arguably the best racehorse ever. At the Kentucky Derby and the Preakness Stakes, Sham came in second to Secretariat. Finally, at the Belmont Stakes Sham started strong and kept pace with Secretariat, but ultimately fell back to last place. Sham was squeezed by the competition and his career was left in shambles.

Thoughts for Reflection

- "When your values are clear to you, making decisions becomes easier." - Roy Disney
- "If you don't listen to your customers, someone else will." - Sam Walton
- "Most people do not listen with intent to understand; they listen with the intent to reply." - Stephen R. Covey
- "In all crises of human affairs there are two broad courses open to a man. He can stay where he is, or he can go elsewhere." - P.G. Wodehouse
- "To be aroused in the dark by five feet of cold, green snake gliding over one's face is unpleasant." - David Livingstone
- "Even snakes are afraid of snakes." - Steven Wright
- "A snake in the grass is deadlier than a lion in a tree." - Matshona Dhliwayo
- "Use your enemy's hand to catch a snake." - Persian Proverb
- "If I seem to take part in politics, it is only because politics encircles us today like the coil of a snake from which one cannot get out, no matter how much one tries. I wish therefore to wrestle with the snake." - Mahatma Gandhi

- "The world of men is dreaming, it has gone mad in its sleep, and a snake is strangling it, but it can't wake up." - D.H. Lawrence
- "Life feels like a game of Snakes and Ladders, but without any ladders." - David Moody
- "In fact, most people are being squeezed in their little cubicles, and their creativity is forced out elsewhere, because the company can't use it. The company is organized to get rid of variants." - Scott Adams
- "The snake kills by squeezing very slowly. This is how the civilized world slowly, slowly pushes into the forest and takes away the world that used to be." - James Cameron
- "I think most human beings, even if you're in a situation that's constricting or complicated or hard, they try to survive." - Maggie Gyllenhaal

Chapter 3: Wolverine

"Life is getting up one more time than you've been knocked down."
- John Wayne

Chapter 3: Wolverine - Absolute Tenacity

Wolverines are voracious scavengers, solitary animals known for their ferocity and strength. In terms of live prey, wolverines pursue smaller, easier to obtain animals. But wolverines have been recorded killing much larger prey such as deer, bison, and moose.

Wolverines and honey badgers are close relatives of weasels. They are fearless and can stand up to even larger animals like lions and even venomous snakes. Put another way, wolverines are the Marines of the animal world.

Colonel Sanders - 1009 Rejections

In 1939, Colonel Sanders started a motel and restaurant which was destroyed by fire just four months later. He rebuilt the motel in 1940 but World War II forced him to close it down. In 1955, once again one of his restaurants failed after an Interstate route changed. In the same year, he was just left with only a $105 social security check to his name.

At the age of 65, he set out to sell his franchised-chicken model to restaurants across the country. He traveled door to door to houses and restaurants all over his local area. He was famously rejected by 1,009 restaurants before one agreed to his idea. He wanted to find someone to help promote his chicken recipe but was faced with a lot of disappointments.

When most people think of retiring, this man set out to share his secret recipe for fried chicken, faced multiple rejections, and finally succeeded.

In 1964, he sold more than 600 franchises with his trademark and sold the Kentucky Fried Chicken corporation for $2 million.

No matter what the obstacle - Keep on keeping on is the model set forth by the wolverine.

"When faced with a mountain, I will not quit! I will keep on striving until I climb over, find a pass through, tunnel underneath, or simply stay and turn the mountain into a gold mine!" - Robert H. Schuller

Adversity is the crucible that shapes and forms us:

- Walt Disney was fired from a newspaper because he "lacked imagination and had no good ideas." His first business, Laugh-O-Grams, ended in bankruptcy.

- Oprah Winfrey, at the age of 22, was fired from her job as a television reporter because she was 'unfit for TV'.

- Steven Spielberg was rejected from USC film school, not once…not twice…but three times.
- Michael Jordan was cut from his high school basketball team.
- Thomas Edison failed some 10,000 times before successfully inventing the light bulb. He viewed it as identifying 10,000 failed experiments.

Alibaba founder Jack Ma is one of the richest people in the world, but there was a time when he couldn't even get a job at Kentucky Fried Chicken. He said, "If you cannot get used to failure - just like a boxer - if you can't get used to [being] hit, how can you win?" I imagine that the Colonel would have agreed.

What led these successful and talented people to continue despite failure and rejection? Some call it GRIT. **We call it the wolverine mindset of tenacity at its finest.**

Application in Life

"Pivot or persevere" is one of the toughest personal questions we consider. Grit is passion and perseverance for long-term and meaningful goals. It is the ability to persist in something you feel passionate about and persevere when you face obstacles. It is mostly mental and the reason only a fraction of Navy Seal candidates makes it through training.

But let us not forget the lesson of the eagle and keeping the big picture in mind. Focus on the goals ahead and have flexible plans in place while you move forward. Have contingency plans in place as you strive to tackle obstacles that get in your way.

Pivoting in life and business is a vital part of the process. "We Cannot Direct the Wind, But We Can Adjust the Sails." - Thomas S. Monson.

"One ship sails East,
And another West,
By the self-same winds that blow,
'Tis the set of the sails And not the gales,
That tells the way we go." - Ella Wheeler Wilcox

Thoughts for Reflection

- "Being defeated is often a temporary condition. Giving up is what makes it permanent." - Marilyn Vos Savant
- "You've got to get up every morning with determination if you're going to go to bed with satisfaction." - George Horace Lorimer
- "He who has a 'why' to live can bear almost any 'how.'" - Friedrich Nietzsche
- "Perhaps there is no more important component of character than steadfast resolution. The boy who is going to make a great man or is going to count in any way in after life, must make up his mind not merely to overcome a thousand obstacles, but to win in spite of a thousand repulses or defeats." - Theodore Roosevelt
- "The most difficult thing is the decision to act, the rest is merely tenacity. The fears are paper tigers. You can do anything you decide to do. You can act to change and control your life; and the procedure, the process is its own reward."- Amelia Earhart
- "Patience and tenacity are worth more than twice their weight of cleverness."- Thomas Huxley
- "I live by two words: tenacity and gratitude."- Henry Winkler
- "Tenacity is not about avoiding being overwhelmed but being indomitable in the face of the overwhelming odds of your venture's failure."- Andy Dunn

- “Being a top performer - whether it's in business or on the athletic field - requires grit and tenacity, as well as the continuous desire to become better.” - Amy Morin
- “I think entrepreneurship is combining a passion with the tenacity to problem solve and the fearlessness to fail.”- Julia Hartz
- “Good, better, best. Never let it rest. 'Til your good is better and your better is best.” - St. Jerome
- “Tenacity is when you follow your heart - when the whole world is screaming to get back into your head.” - Sonia Choquette
- “Let me tell you the secret that has led me to my goal. My strength lies solely in my tenacity.” - Louis Pasteur
- “Tenacity isn’t just the most important thing, it’s the only thing.” - Mavis Leno
- “Our greatest glory is not never failing, but in rising up every time we fail.” - Ralph Waldo Emerson

Chapter 4: Hippo

"Real difficulties can be overcome-but it's the imaginary ones that are unconquerable."-Theodore N. Vail

Chapter 4 Hippo - Territorial

Hippos are among the most dangerous animals in the world due to their highly aggressive and unpredictable nature. After elephants and rhinoceros, the hippopotamus is the third largest land animal. They will defend their water and land territories and have been known to tear apart lions with their enormous teeth and jaws.

Hippos can run faster than humans on land and swim faster than humans in water. Which means a motorized vehicle may be your only chance of outdistancing a hippo.

Hippos in business are very territorial. In fact, they try to corner markets by eliminating competition. It is very difficult and ill advised to try and compete directly against the hippos that think they own the territory. Business hippos have the advantage because they have significant market power. They become the exclusive supplier of a commodity or service, thus creating a monopoly.

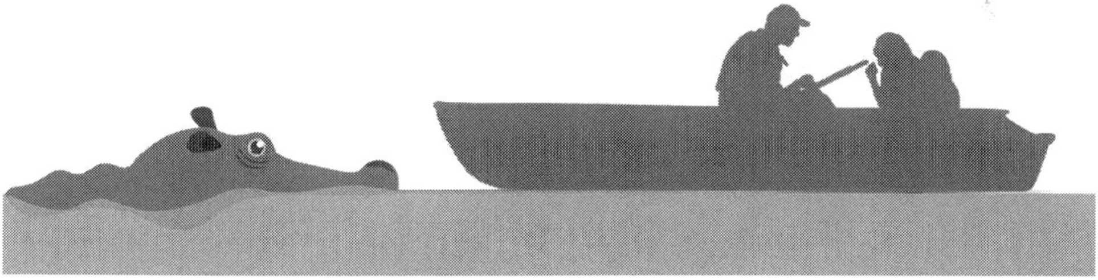

The Monopolist

By 1880, just 10 years after its founding, John D Rockefeller's Standard Oil owned or controlled 90 percent of the U.S. oil refining business, making it the first great industrial monopoly in the world.

The company prospered and began to buy out its competitors rapidly. It acquired pipelines and terminal facilities, purchased competing refineries in other cities, and vigorously expanded its markets. It kept oil prices low to stave off competitors. Its maze of legal structures made it virtually impervious to public investigation.

By 1882, the Ohio Supreme Court ordered the trust dissolved, but it effectively continued to operate from headquarters in New Jersey.

A few years later in 1901 oil was discovered at Spindletop Hill in Beaumont, Texas. An antitrust suit prevented Standard Oil from capitalizing on its find. Moreover, an oil products marketing firm affiliated with Standard Oil was banned from conducting business in the state of Texas. Finally, Standard Oil was able to build refineries in the area, but it was unable to dominate in Texas the way it had in the Eastern states.

Applications

It's tough to compete directly against entrenched competitors and monopolies in life and business. Instead, find where people's needs are not being met and try to fill those. Often, we need to create a need and then fill it.

In any career, find where there are problems and solve them. One of my first jobs at age 16 was selling Fuller Brushes. I discovered that if I asked customers "what else can I help you with?" they would tell me. I would take the orders, fulfill them, and bring back the receipts to my regional supervisor. Within months I was promoted to a regional position.

When running a business, find the opportunities where big and entrenched competitors are not. Competing in an undifferentiated commodity business with a "me too" strategy is a recipe for failure.

We need to make it easy for others to hire us or to do business with us. Find out what it takes to help them be successful. Create a plan to help them achieve their goals and then...Bingo! We have a new customer or a new job. There is now an opportunity for great things ahead.

Thoughts for Reflection

- "It's not the strongest of the species that survives, nor the most intelligent, but the one most adaptable to change." - Charles Darwin

- "All happy companies are different: each one earns a monopoly by solving a unique problem. All failed companies are the same: they failed to escape competition." - Peter Thiel.
- "The greater the power, the more dangerous the abuse." - Edmund Burke

- "Power tends to corrupt and absolute power corrupts absolutely." - John Dalberg-Acton

- "The biggest competition is myself. I am not looking to follow others or pull them down. I'm planning to test my own boundaries." - Rain

- "I am neither of the East nor of the West, no boundaries exist within my breast." - Rumi

- "Hippos' ferocity is legendary; they kill more people than any other mammal." - Tom Hennigan

- "If a hippo ever wants to fight, just walk away." - Dan Brown

- "The illiterate of the future will not be the person who cannot read. It will be the person who does not know how to learn." - Alvin Toffler

- “A man flattened by an opponent can get up again. A man flattened by conformity stays down for good.” - Thomas J. Watson, Jr.

- “I think it's wrong that only one company makes the game Monopoly.” - Steve Wright

- “A woman is like a tea bag - you can't tell how strong she is until you put her in hot water.” - Eleanor Roosevelt

- “The only thing necessary for the triumph of evil is for good men to do nothing.” - Edmund Burke

- “Honest disagreement is often a good sign of progress.” - Mahatma Gandhi

- “Good judgment comes from experience, and a lot of that comes from bad judgment.” - Will Rogers

Chapter 5: Lion

"A lion sleeps in the heart of every brave man."
-Turkish Proverb

Chapter 5: Lion - Courage Under Pressure

African lions have been admired throughout history as symbols of courage and strength. The lion is not the biggest, the strongest nor the fastest in the animal kingdom. But it is the king because it is the most courageous.

"Courage is rightly esteemed the first of human qualities because it has been said, it is the quality which guarantees all others." - Winston Churchill

The Hero

Courageous people feel fear but do it anyway. They inspire us to become better versions of ourselves. Psychologist Scott T. Allison notes, "They call us to become heroes too". In other words, heroes are leaders.

On 9/11 when two jets collided into the World Trade Towers, Rick Rescorla, a Vietnam veteran, and disaster planner, was credited with saving the lives of 2,687 Morgan Stanley employees and 250 office visitors. When he safely had them outside, he went back in to save more. He was one of only 13 Morgan Stanley employees who died on that day.

Remember the cowardly lion from the Wizard of Oz? "We eventually learn that he's not really a coward; rather, the Lion thinks he is because he doesn't believe in himself. By the end of the film, the Cowardly Lion performs several courageous acts without realizing his bravery." - Simran Khurana

Application in Life

Courage is what separates the lions from the sheep. Honesty, integrity, and determination would not exist without courage. Courage is the foundation upon which all great leadership is built.

Some people play "not to lose" while others "play to win". I personally believe that a good offense is the best defense. The next time you have a fear of something, ask yourself "What are the true risks of failure?" You may discover your fears are exaggerated. Take some time to identify your fear. It may take courage to face it but avoiding it can make it even scarier.

"The price of success is much lower than the price of failure." - Zig Ziglar

There are risks to inaction. The young man might be afraid to ask the young woman on a date because he is afraid of rejection. But not asking ensures the date will never happen. Maybe you want a new job or promotion. Perhaps you want to refinance your house?

Overcoming a fear can be quite liberating. Fear whether imagined or irrational must be overcome. If we let fear control our lives, then we limit our ability to move forward or to live life to its fullest potential. Instead of focusing on the fear, focus on trying to build courage. You build self-confidence and resilience by developing courage. Adopt a growth mindset. Create a compelling goal. Remember that no one is perfect and there may be failures along the way. Try different approaches and truly commit. You can break through your fear barriers to move one step closer to achieving your goals. This is courage in action.

"You miss 100% of the shots you don't take." - Wayne Gretzky

Nike - the Goddess of Victory

In 1964, Phil Knight teamed with his former Oregon track coach Bob Bowerman, and with $500 each they formed Blue Ribbon Sports. The company initially operated as a distributor for Japanese shoemaker Onitsuka Tiger, making most of its sales at track meets out of the trunk of Knight's car. Today we know the company as Nike.

"Phil Knight's memoir "Shoe Dog" is a refreshingly honest reminder

of what the path to business success really looks like. It's a messy, perilous, and chaotic journey riddled with mistakes, endless struggles, and sacrifice. In fact, the only thing that seems inevitable...is that it will end in failure." - Bill Gates

At the end of his memoir Knight said, "God, how I wish I could relive the whole thing." It's no wonder that Nike's slogan is "Just Do It".

Application in Career and Business

Author Brene Brown views leadership as "having the courage to communicate that you don't have all the answers, having the ability to see the potential in others and having the curiosity to seek out those who can help solve a problem."

It takes courage to be vulnerable or admit that you are wrong. My company had stopped growing so we brought in an organizational development consultant, an Industrial Psychologist. He helped us to understand that the problem was with our leadership - namely me and my partner. He forced us to face and recognize the problems, which caused us to introduce change. After some much needed tweaks we were able to start growing again.

Thoughts for Reflection

- "Courage is being scared to death - but saddling up anyway." - John Wayne

- “The fact is that my appetite for risk was far greater than that of other people, and my courage in my own conviction was unshakable.” - Sheldon Adelson

- “Wars may be fought with weapons, but they are won by men. It is the spirit of the men who follow and of the man who leads that gained the victory.” - George S. Patton

- “Fear...is forward. No one is afraid of yesterday.” - Renata Adler

- “Courage is the fear of holding on a minute longer.” - George S. Patton

- “Death is not the enemy, living in constant fear of it is.” - Norman Cousins

- “Life is either a daring adventure or nothing.” - Helen Keller

- “Good ideas are not adopted automatically. They must be driven into practice with courageous impatience.” - Hyman Rickover

- “If we want to succeed…then we better look like we mean business. Things do not happen. Things are made to happen.”- John F. Kennedy
- “Letting the cat outta the bag is a whole lot easier than putting it back. “- Will Rogers
- “Only those who will risk going too far can possibly find out how far one can go.”- TS Eliot
- “Courage is resistance to fear, mastery of fear, not absence of fear.” - Mark Twain
- “The harder the conflict, the more glorious the triumph. What we obtain too cheap, we esteem too lightly; it is dearness only that gives everything its value. I love the man that can smile in trouble, that can gather strength from distress and grow brave.” - Thomas Paine
- “Courage is fire, and bullying is smoke.” - Benjamin Disraeli
- “Your time is limited, so don't waste it living someone else's life…and most important, have the courage to follow your heart and intuition.” - Steve Jobs

Chapter 6: Elephant

"When there is an invisible elephant in the room, one is from time to time bound to trip over a trunk."

- Karen Joy Fowler

Chapter 6: Elephant - In the Room

Elephants are big. They are the largest land animal weighing up to 15,000 pounds. An elephant's trunk has up to 40,000 muscles whereas humans have just 639 muscles in their entire body. Elephants use their trunks to help them suck up water for drinking, picking up or touching objects, trumpeting warnings, and greeting one another.

Elephant and Blind Men

As the parable goes, blind men were asked to describe an elephant. The first man who felt the trunk, said, "This being is like a snake". Another touching the animal's ear described a fan. The man, whose hand was upon its leg, said, the elephant is a pillar like a tree-trunk. The one who placed his hand upon its side said to the elephant, "is a wall". Another who felt its tail, described it as a rope. The last felt its tusk, stating the elephant is that which is hard, smooth and like a spear.

Government is the elephant in the room

The elephant and the government are big, powerful, and call the shots. Governments affect taxes, laws, regulation, government spending and supply of money. They are big and beyond most of our abilities to understand let alone control or predict. The same is true of economic cycles.

According to Warren Buffet "Listening to market predictions of others is a waste of time. It's dangerous because it may blur your vision of the facts that are truly important."

During one recession, we created a banner that greeted people entering our lobby with "We understand that there is a recession but have chosen not to participate." This attitude resonated with our employees. Our company continued to grow during that time. "Attitudes are caught, not taught." Alexander the Great

Government spending accounts for over 40% of our economy and that is a large percentage! Two-thirds of that spending is not up for debate. Of the remaining third, defense spending is about $700 billion and is "discretionary". In our world there is not much we can do about it.

The lesson from the elephant is that we cannot keep others from kicking us...But we can determine the direction we go once we have been kicked.

Thoughts for Reflection

- "In matters of style, swim with the current; in matters of principle, stand like a rock." - Thomas Jefferson

- "Too bad that all the people who know how to run the country are busy driving taxicabs and cutting hair." - George Burns

- "The single most exciting thing you encounter in government is competence, because it's so rare." - Sen. Daniel Patrick Moynihan

- "When stupidity is considered patriotism, it is unsafe to be intelligent." - Isaac Asimov

- "Potentially, a government is the most dangerous threat to man's rights: it holds a legal monopoly on the use of physical force against legally disarmed victims." - Ayn Rand

- "Experience hath shewn, that even under the best forms, those entrusted with power have, in time, and by slow operations, perverted it into tyranny." - Thomas Jefferson

- "If size mattered, the elephant would be the king of the jungle." - Rickson Gracie

- "The only barrier to human development is ignorance, and this is not insurmountable."- Robert H. Goddard

- “When you're right, no one remembers. When you're wrong nobody forgets.” - Muhammad Ali

- “When eating an elephant, take one bite at a time.” - Creighton Abrams

- “When you have got an elephant by the hind legs and he is trying to run away, it's best to let him run.” - Abraham Lincoln

- “I have a memory like an elephant. I remember every elephant I've ever met.” - Herb Caen

- “God grant me the Serenity to accept the things I cannot change, the Courage to change the things I can, and the Wisdom to know the difference.” - Reinhold Niebuhr

- “A government big enough to give you everything you want is a government big enough to take from you everything you have.” - Gerald R. Ford

- “Nationalism is an infantile disease. It is the measles of mankind.” - Albert Einstein

Chapter 7: Gorilla

Remember when you are at the dance with a gorilla, you are not done dancing until the gorilla is…

Chapter 7: Gorilla - The Dictator

Gorillas are the largest living primates and tend to live in troops with one mature male as the leader and multiple females and offspring. The silverback makes all decisions, mediates conflicts, determines group movements, and takes responsibility for the safety and wellbeing of the troop.

Dancing with the Gorilla

Gorillas represent those relationships in our lives where one party has a lot of power…and tends to abuse it. You might be a spouse that feels trapped in an unhealthy marriage. Or you might feel trapped in a demanding job that you don't like. You might have an unreasonable boss or employer. You might feel owned by your business.

Application in Life

We are often trapped by our beliefs, fears, and feelings. Perhaps we believe that our partner will change or that we are the only one who can help them. We might fear making major life changes. We may even harbor feelings of responsibility for being abused, helpless, and isolated. Whatever the case may be, it's no fun and often unhealthy dancing with a gorilla.

Application at Work

According to a recent study by TopResume, 96 percent of professionals have felt bullied at work, with 71 percent feeling bullied by a boss. Twenty five percent acknowledge dealing with toxic co-workers. Unfortunately, this is common. My advice is to continue learning. Gain skill sets that improve your mobility that don't make you reliant on any employer or boss.

Application in Business

If you are a business owner, you may feel trapped by your obligations - delivering work, meeting payroll, paying suppliers and the IRS. You might even feel that your business owns you.

You might have one big customer or distributor who has excessive control over your destiny. The negotiation power that Walmart has over its suppliers is legendary. Get into Walmart and you may have access to over 10,500 stores worldwide. Play well with them and they will give you prime shelf space. But getting into Walmart comes at a price.

Dealing with the Gorilla

There are several strategies for dealing with gorillas. The first is to recognize that most relationships are "at will" and that the true enemy is fear. You will need to take responsibility for those parts of the relationship you can control. It might mean learning new things and growing. Perhaps you find a way to take yourself out of the situation. You will need to develop mental toughness. Directly address the issue or the individual gorilla. They may not give you the same courtesy but, they might understand your viewpoint.

If you run a business, it might mean getting new customers or diversifying your distribution and supplier bases.

Thoughts for Reflection

- "I believe in benevolent dictatorship provided I am the dictator." - Richard Branson
- "Every dictator is an enemy of freedom, an opponent of law." - Demosthenes
- "You do not teach the paths of the forest to an old gorilla." African Proverb
- "The 800-pound gorilla just entered the blogosphere with Google launching its blog search." - Charlene Li
- "Abuse of power comes as no surprise." - Jenny Holzer
- "Abuse of power isn't limited to bad guys in other nations. It happens in our own country if we're not vigilant." - Clint Eastwood
- "You don't lead by hitting people on the head. That's assault, not leadership." - Dwight D. Eisenhower
- "It's not just the abuse of power that's the problem. It's the power to abuse." - Stefan Molyneux
- "The greater the power, the more dangerous the abuse." - Edmund Burke

- “Apes beat their chests, so they don’t have to fight 24 hours a day.” - David Milch
- “Gorillas are very intelligent, but they don’t have to be as delicate as chimps — they can just smash open the termite nest.” - Richard Carroll
- “Clothes make the man. Naked people have little or no influence on society.” - Mark Twain
- “When it comes to tyrants, dictators and terrorists, strength and the threat of force is the only language they understand.” - Kevin McCarthy
- “Democracy consists of choosing your dictators, after they've told you what you think it is you want to hear.” - Alan Coren
- “Ignorance is an evil weed, which dictators may cultivate among their dupes, but which no democracy can afford among its citizens.” - William Beveridge
- “This and no other is the root from which a tyrant springs; when he first appears, he is a protector.” - Plato
- “How strangely will the Tools of a Tyrant pervert the plain Meaning of Words!” - Samuel Adams

Chapter 8: Owl

Proper training will teach us what to do… but a good education and the application of some common sense will teach us what to be!
Wisdom of the Owl

Chapter 8: Owl - Wisdom from Reflection

Owls are nocturnal birds of prey and are considered symbols of wisdom due to their successful hunting strategies of stealth and surprise. They are sometimes known as "Eagles of the night".

Most owls share an innate ability to fly almost silently and more slowly in comparison to other birds of prey. Being able to fly without making any noise gives them a strong advantage over their prey that are listening for any sign of noise in the dark night. With large light gathering retinas, they can virtually see in the dark and have nocturnal eyesight to be far superior to that of its average prey.

The Netflix story - A Wise Decision

Reed Hastings has said the idea for Netflix was sparked by a $40 fine he got for renting the movie Apollo 13 from Blockbuster and returning it six weeks late. While working out at the gym one day, the sting from the fine inspired him to think up a service that allowed one to order a movie DVD online and get it by mail.

Today, Netflix is one of the world's leading entertainment services with $30 billion in revenue, 222 million paid memberships in over 190 countries enjoying TV series, documentaries, feature films and mobile games across a wide variety of genres and languages.

Netflix proposed in 2000 that Blockbuster should use Netflix as its online service and Blockbuster "nearly laughed us out of the office", recalled Netflix's former CFO. Today Blockbuster is no longer in business.

Brian Tracy has said that "Wisdom comes from experience with reflection". The Netflix story is where one person's negative experience was transformed by his reflection into an amazing opportunity.

The Story of the Owl and Frog

The frog is sitting on a lily pad out in the middle of a pond. And the owl is perched on a limb hanging out over the pond. The owl sees the frog and asks, "Hey Mr. Frog, how are you doing?" The frog replies "I'm not doing so well. You know, I'm stuck out here on the lily pad in the middle of a pond and there are crocodiles all around. I wish I could fly like you and go anywhere."

The owl says, "It's easy, just back up a little bit on that lily pad. Flap your legs together, jump, and fly out of that pond. So, the frog says "Well Mr. Owl that's a pretty good idea. I think I'll do that. So, he backs up on the lily pad, flaps his legs together and takes a jump but ends up in the pond. Along comes a Crocodile. The frog looks up and says, "Hey you stupid owl, frogs can't fly." The owl replies, "Listen Mr. Frog, I only deal in concepts; it's your job to implement."

Application

Life gives us many opportunities to reflect on our direct experiences and those that happen to those around us. We can question why certain relationships are working and why others are not. We can reflect on our attitudes and beliefs. Keeping a journal is an amazing way to write down and process what we are experiencing. Trevor Blake has started three $100 million plus companies with no employees. He will tell you that journaling in the morning is one of the most important things he does.

Thoughts for Reflection

- "By three methods we may learn wisdom: First, by reflection, which is noblest; Second, by imitation, which is easiest; and third by experience, which is the bitterest."- Confucius

- "The least of things with a meaning is worth more in life than the greatest of things without it." - Carl Jung

- "The mind, once stretched by a new idea, never returns to its original dimensions." - Ralph Waldo Emerson

- "Great minds discuss ideas. Average minds discuss events. Small minds discuss people." - Eleanor Roosevelt

- "Mistakes are the usual bridge between inexperience and wisdom." - Phyllis Theroux

- "Who looks outside, dreams, who looks inside, awakes." - Carl Jung

- "There is always a well-known solution to every human problem - neat, plausible, and wrong." - H.L. Mencken

- "Insanity is doing the same thing over and over again, expecting different results." - Albert Einstein

- "All wish to possess knowledge, but few, comparatively speaking, are willing to pay the price." - Juvenal

- “It’s not that I’m so smart, it’s just that I stay with problems longer.” - Albert Einstein

- “Good people are good because they’ve come to wisdom through failure. We get very little wisdom from success, you know.” - William Saroyan

- “Some men never find the key to success because they don’t look in the right place – inside their own minds.” - B.C. Forbes
- “Life can only be understood backwards; but it must be lived forwards.”- Soren Kierkegaard
- “The only source of knowledge is experience.”- Albert Einstein
- “Experience is the teacher of all things.”- Julius Caesar
- “Practice does not make perfect. Only perfect practice makes perfect.”- Vince Lombardi
- “The only true wisdom is in knowing you know nothing.”- Socrates
- “The wisest mind has something yet to learn.” - George Santayana

Chapter 9: Piranha

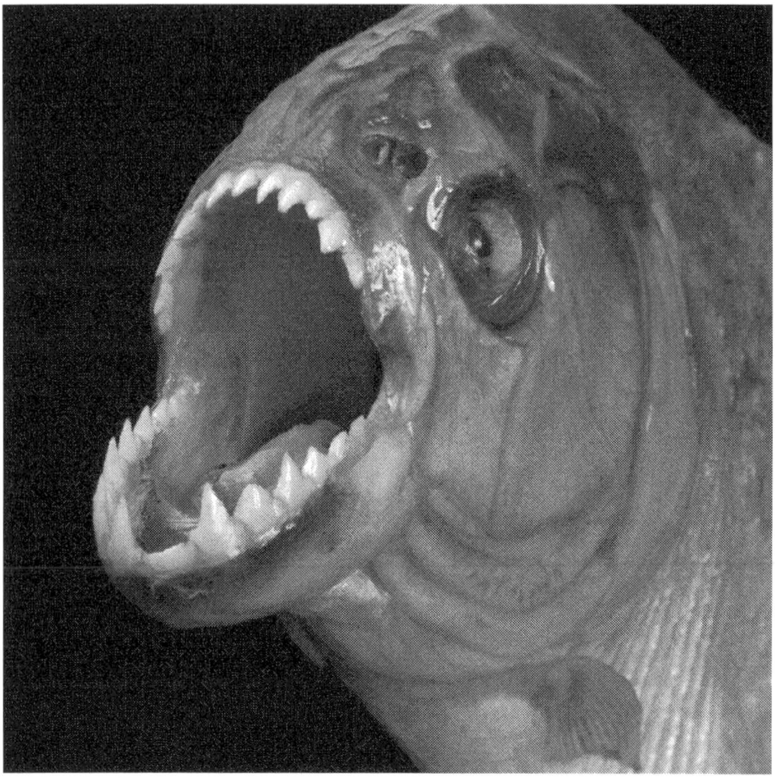

"Don't be distracted by criticism. Remember the only taste of success some people have is when they take a bite out of you."
- Zig Ziglar

Chapter 9: Piranha - Death by a Thousand Nibbles

The piranha or "tooth fish" is known for its razor-sharp teeth and relentless bite. Piranhas tend to attack dead meat more than live animals. Humans are viewed more as a source of danger than prey. But piranhas will attack if stressed or provoked. Schools of piranha will bind together as a means of defense against predators.

Banking institution nickel and dimed its clients

One bank customer in Northern California discovered that he had seven additional accounts that he did not consent to. According to his lawsuit, his credit score had suffered because unpaid fees on the unauthorized accounts had been sent to a debt collector.

In all, banking employees of the institution opened roughly 1.5 million bank accounts and applied for 565,000 credit cards that may not have been authorized by customers. These illegal banking practices would cost this company $185 million in fines, including a $100 million penalty from the Consumer Financial Protection Bureau, the largest such penalty the agency has issued. The bank fired at least 5,300 employees who were involved.

The fraud appears to have stemmed from the CEO's mantra to employees: "Eight is great." Meaning: get eight bank products into the hands of each customer.

Death by a Thousand Bites

Piranhas represent situations where we die one small bite at a time. It has been claimed that frogs will slowly boil to death if thrown into water when the heat is turned up gradually. Metaphorically, a piranha might be a negative environment, bad habit or even debt where one is diminished over time.

It might be a physically challenging or unhealthy environment. Coal miners often contracted "black lung" from inhaling coal dust. Restaurant workers had been exposed to secondhand smoke. Bad ergonomics might promote carpal tunnel syndrome.

It's a fact that many dentists need to retire early from back issues they have acquired from working in awkward positions. There is evidence that sitting at a desk for long periods of time can promote diabetes and heart disease.

Applications

Consider the long-term implications of short-term thinking. Realize that there are tradeoffs and that you have only one body.

Twenty years ago, my doctor told me that if I didn't change my life and reduce stress that I would not live but just a couple years more. It was the daily bites from the piranhas in the world that caused all the stress. This contributed to my high blood pressure and ultimately caused kidney failure.

I sold my half of the business to my former partner and received a new kidney, compliments of my son Jason. With that I got a new lease on life.

Habits matter. Identify the cue or trigger event for your habits. Write out a new routine and give yourself a reward when you successfully complete it. Eat well and exercise regularly. If you can't care or respect yourself, how can you expect others to do so?

Thoughts for Reflection

- “Our lives begin to end the day we become silent about things that matter.” - Martin Luther King Jr.

- “The world is a dangerous place. Not because of the people who are evil, but because of the people who don’t do anything about it.” - Albert Einstein

- “I dream of a better tomorrow, where chickens can cross the road and not be questioned about their motives.” - Ralph Waldo Emerson

- “A people that values its privileges above its principles soon loses both.” - Dwight D. Eisenhower

- “It is easier to prevent bad habits than to break them.” - Benjamin Franklin

- “A change in bad habits leads to a change in life.” - Jenny Craig

- “What studies say the number one best way to start an exercise habit is to give yourself a reward that you genuinely enjoy.” - Charles Duhigg

- “Better to be an optimist who gets disappointed than a pessimist who has no hope.” - Robin S. Sharma

- “You don’t have to attend every argument to which you are invited.” - Unknown

- The key to winning our position is to “Use soft words and hard arguments”. - English Proverb

- “Remember not only to say the right thing in the right place, but far more difficult still, to leave unsaid the wrong thing at the tempting moment.” - Benjamin Franklin
- “Always do right. This will gratify some people and astonish the rest.” - Mark Twain
- “Men who try to do something and fail are infinitely better than those who try to do nothing and succeed.” - Lloyd Jones
- “The eyes can choose where to look, but the ears cannot choose where to listen.” - Ursula K. Le Guin
- “Put your heart, mind, and soul into even your smallest acts. This is the secret of success.” - Swami Sivananda
- “When nothing seems to help, I go and look at a stonecutter hammering away at his rock, perhaps a hundred times without as much as a crack showing in it. Yet at the hundred and first blow it will split in two, and I know it was not that blow that did it – but all that had gone before.” - Jacob Riis

Chapter 10: Dog

A dog can teach us unconditional love.
If we can have that in our life…things won't be too bad.

Chapter 10: Dog - Loyalty and Serving Others

Dogs are naturally loving and affectionate animals. They develop strong bonds with those they perceive as members of their pack. And packs succeed because the members depend on one another to survive. A dog that seeks to dominate may use aggression to elevate its power and authority within the pack.

Stories on Man's Best Friend

Morgan Cutolo recently compiled some stories of "man's best friend" in Reader's Digest. Here are a few examples:

After my 12-year-old son passed away from leukemia, my husband brought home a collie puppy that we named Charlie. At first, I resented how full of life he was, but I slowly started to warm up to him. He would jump up on me and bark, and if I ever became angry, he would lick my face. He helped me get out of bed and get back to normal. He would go skiing with my husband, play with my son, and was a great companion to my dad. Therapy was recommended for my family after my son died, but we didn't need it, we had Charlie. - Charlene Wexler

When I fell on a slippery grassy slope, I lost hold of my beloved Duffie's leash. In spite of his freedom, he stayed by my side, barking for someone to come to my aid. Duffie died at the age of seventeen and would have lived longer, had I not, as my final act of love, had him put down. That was in 2001. There's not a day that goes by that I don't miss my super dog. - Bonnie Hannes

My sister is a psychologist, and her dog Dutch sits in on her sessions. If tension arises between spouses, he immediately gets up from his sleeping position and goes back and forth between man and woman nosing their hands until they reach out to pet him. Tension is released immediately. He truly is an emotional support dog. - Diana Herkimer

Dogs are guardians

Metaphorically, dogs are loyal guardians of our households and traditions. They are protective of our friends and families and vigilant against potential threats and intruders.

Owning a dog can help you live longer. Studies have found that dog owners have lower blood pressure levels and improved responses to stress. My dog Molly keeps me company at work every day. She helps me stay calm in many hectic situations.

Application in Life

"The best way to find yourself is to lose yourself in the service of others." - Gandhi

Serving others can be a source of great joy and meaning. And being surrounded by good friends will enhance your life as well. Care providers such as nurses and doctors are our heroes day in and day out.

I believe that relationships are everything and having good ones will increase the quality of your life. Guard your friends and family - watch their backs.

My friend Zig Ziglar often said, "You can have everything you want in life if you help enough other people get what they want."

This is true in both life and business. I have been fortunate enough to have quite a few long-term relationships. Frequently, an old friend will reach out to me wondering how I am doing. Sometimes they tell me about a project they need help with.

Never underestimate the value of investing time and sharing real experiences. Nowadays so many rely on social media to communicate. Strong bonds are not nurtured and maintained by Facebook. Pick up the phone and call someone. Send a note or a thoughtful card. I appreciate a written card over a hastily sent text or meme any day.

Thoughts for Reflection

- "If you would win a man to your cause, first convince him you are his sincere friend." - Abraham Lincoln

- "The respect of those you respect is worth more than the applause of the multitude." - Arnold Glasow

- "Hatred always corrodes the container it's carried in." - Alan Simpson

- "Dogs come when they are called; cats take a message and get back to you later." - Mary Bly

- "Heaven goes by favor. If it went by merit, your dog would go in and you would stay out." - Mark Twain
- "Our rewards in life will always be in exact proportion to the amount of consideration we show toward others." - Earl Nightingale
- "The most important ingredient we put into any relationship is not what we say or what we do, but what we are." - Stephen R. Covey
- "The secret of a good life is to have the right loyalties and hold them in the right scale of values." - Norman Thomas
- "Trust but verify." - Ronald Reagan

- “Walking with a friend in the dark is better than walking alone in the light.” - Helen Keller
- “One of the most beautiful qualities of true friendship is to understand and to be understood.” - Lucius Annaeus Seneca
- “It is one of the blessings of old friends that you can afford to be stupid with them.” - Ralph Waldo Emerson
- “Lots of people want to ride with you in the limo, but what you want is someone who will take the bus with you when the limo breaks down.” - Oprah Winfrey
- “Honesty and loyalty are key. If two people can be honest with each other about everything, that's probably the biggest key to success.” - Taylor Lautner
- “Confidentiality is a virtue of the loyal, as loyalty is the virtue of faithfulness.” - Edwin Louis Cole
- “You cannot escape the responsibility of tomorrow by evading it today.” - Abraham Lincoln
- “Whoever is careless with the truth in small matters cannot be trusted with important matters.” - Albert Einstein
- “Three things cannot be long hidden: the sun, the moon, and the truth.”- Buddha

Chapter 11: Zebra

"I've had many worries in my life.
Most of which have never happened."
- Mark Twain

Chapter 11: Zebra - Leaving Worry at the Waterhole

Zebras are far more aggressive than horses and have several modes of self-defense. They defend their herd and territory by kicking, biting, and pushing enemies. When threatened, these African equines escape larger predators by fleeing. If speed is not enough, zebras will turn sideways, especially when the predator is close behind. Finally, the black and white stripes help to keep them camouflaged.

Zebras don't worry

According to Dr. Robert Sapolsky, author of "Why Zebras Don't Get Ulcers", zebras handle stress well and we can learn a lot from them. Chronic stress has become one of the leading causes of death, leading to strokes, heart attacks and kidney failure. It is also related to loss of immunity, insomnia, anxiety, depression, addiction, obesity, heart disease, and serious memory loss.

Zebras don't usually stress out about things like humans do but rather focus on physical stressors like lions. In other words, zebras live in the moment. They don't worry. Nor do they worry until they see a lion coming towards them. In other words, they don't worry until it's time to worry. Then they spring into action.

Application

Dale Carnegie says in the preface to "How to Stop Worrying and Start Living" that he wrote it because he "was one of the unhappiest lads in New York". The book he wrote is a classic. Here is a summary of his seven ways to cultivate a great mental attitude:

1. Fill your mind with the right thoughts. The outcome of your life reflects your thoughts.

2. Never try to get even with your enemies. When you try to get even with your enemies, you hurt yourself more than them.

3. Don't worry about ingratitude. Expect it. The only way to find happiness is through the joy of giving.

4. Be grateful for what you have. "Count your blessings, not your problems." - Roy T. Bennett

5. "Be your best self and do not imitate others." - Robert Smith

6. Make the best out of every situation. "When fate hands you lemons, make lemonade." - Dale Carnegie

7. "Some pursue happiness, others create it." - Ralph Waldo Emerson

Thoughts for Reflection

- "You wouldn't worry so much about what others think of you if you realized how seldom they do" - Eleanor Roosevelt.
- "Don't Worry, Be Happy." - Bobby McFerrin
- "Worrying is like a rocking chair, it gives you something to do, but it gets you nowhere."- Erma Bombeck
- "If it can be solved, there's no need to worry, and if it can't be solved, worry is of no use." - Dalai Lama XIV
- "Don't worry about failure. Worry about the chances you miss when you don't even try." - Jack Canfield
- "Worry often gives a small thing a big shadow." - Swedish Proverb
- "Know when to hold 'em, know when to fold 'em, know when to walk away, and know when to run." - Kenny Rogers
- "Worry never climbed a hill, Worry never paid a bill, Worry never dried a tear, Worry never calmed a fear, Worry never darned a heel, Worry never cooked a meal, Worry never led a horse to water Worry never done a thing you'd think it oughta." - Jo Petty, *Apples of Gold*
- "Stop worrying about what can go wrong and get excited about what can go right." - Anonymous

- “Worrying does not take away tomorrow’s troubles, it takes away today’s peace.” - Zig Ziglar
- “Our fatigue is often caused not by work, but by worry, frustration, and resentment.” - Dale Carnegie
- “Do not anticipate trouble or worry about what may never happen. Keep in the sunlight.” - Benjamin Franklin
- “When I look back on all these worries, I remember the story of the old man who said on his deathbed that he had a lot of trouble in his life, most of which never happened.” - Winston Churchill
- “Worry that no one knows you: seek to be worth knowing.” - Confucius
- “It is not work that kills men; it is worry. Worry is rust upon the blade.” - Henry Ward Beecher
- “Do not worry about your difficulties in Mathematics. I can assure you mine are still greater.” - Albert Einstein
- “Whatever is going to happen will happen, whether we worry or not.” - Ana Monnar

Chapter 12: Beaver

"A dream doesn't become reality through magic;
it takes sweat, determination, and hard work."
- Colin Powell

Chapter 12: Beaver - Work Hard...Work Smart

Beavers are smart and industrious. They are large rodents who use their chisel-like incisors to gnaw through wood. Beavers build dams across streams to create a pond where they can build a "beaver lodge" to live in. These ponds provide protection from predators like wolves, coyotes, and mountain lions. It's no wonder that engineering schools like MIT and Caltech have adopted this animal as their mascot.

Beavers represent the values of working hard and smart. Hard work is probably one of the most overlooked core values. The problem is that hard work looks like work. Hard work may not seem glamorous, but it is at the heart of every successful relationship and career.

Henry Ford - The Industrialist

Henry Ford, founder of Ford Motor Company, was an American industrialist, business magnate, and chief developer of the assembly line technique of mass production. By creating the first automobile that middle-class Americans could afford, he converted the automobile from an expensive luxury item into an accessible conveyance that profoundly impacted the landscape of the 20th century.

Henry Ford embodied the notions of working both hard and smart. He believed that "Nothing is particularly hard if you divide it into small jobs." He developed the assembly line concept. In other words, he made work smarter by breaking it into smaller components. Automobile parts where added in sequence from workstation to workstation until the vehicles were finally assembled. McDonald's would do the same in fast food.

Do not confuse activity with accomplishment

Newton defined work as a "force across a distance". If you apply force (energy) to an object but the object does not move, Sir Issac would tell you that no work happened. As a contractor, we would build things and it is very gratifying to see a new project completed. It is the fruits of our labors.

Applications in Life and Business

"Without effort, your talent is nothing more than unmet potential. Without effort, your skill is nothing more than what you could have done but didn't." - Angela Duckworth

Hard work is the key to both success and self-satisfaction. When we do hard work, we can achieve our goals, which leads to self-satisfaction.

"Genius is one percent inspiration and 99 percent perspiration." Thomas Edison understood that innovation involves more than just great ideas. It requires hard work. He used to work 21 hours a day and sleep for 3 hours.

Tools make work easier, and it is a good idea to learn them. Levers were used in ancient Egypt to help workmen uplift obelisks weighing more than 100 tons. Wheels were invented around the same time and allowed for the transport of heavy items. Today we have computers, robots, calendars, and other tools to make our work easier. Become proficient in the tools of your trade because they will leverage you.

Thoughts for Reflection

- "Keep buggering on." - Winston Churchill

- "Obstacles are those frightful things you see when you take your eyes off your goal." - Henry Ford

- "Opportunity is missed by most people because it is dressed in overalls and looks like work." - Thomas Edison

- "Procrastination is opportunity's natural assassin." - Victor Kiam

- "Timing, perseverance and ten years of trying will eventually make you look like an overnight success." - Biz Stone, co-founder of Twitter

- "Everything comes to him who hustles while he waits." - Thomas Edison

- "Knowing is not enough; we must apply. Willing is not enough; we must do." - Goethe

- "There is no try...only do." - Yoda, Star Wars

- "Far and away the best prize that life offers is the chance to work hard at work worth doing." - Theodore Roosevelt

- "Conviction is worthless unless it is converted into conduct." - Thomas Carlyle

- "I never dreamed about success. I worked for it." - Estee Lauder
- "Work like there is someone working twenty-four hours a day to take it from you." - Mark Cuban
- "Success in business requires training and discipline and hard work." - David Rockefeller
- "Focused hard work is the real key to success." - John Carmack
- "Hard work and determination equal success. Nothing comes easy. Put your mind to something." - Kevin Hart
- "Believe in yourself, work hard, work smart and passionately present your best self to the world."- Hill Harper
- "Hard work is the price we must pay for success." - Vince Lombardi
- "Luck is a dividend of sweat. The more you sweat, the luckier you get." - Ray Kroc
- "Diamonds are nothing more than chunks of coal that stuck to their jobs." - Malcolm Forbes
- "Success is not final; failure is not fatal; it is the courage to continue that counts." – Winston Churchill

Chapter 13: Bear

"The gypsies believe the bear to be a brother to man because he has the same body beneath his hide, because he drinks beer, because he enjoys music and because he likes to dance."
- Ernest Hemingway

Chapter 13: Bear - Creative Adaptability

With some minor exceptions, bears have large torsos, stocky legs, narrow snouts, long hair, short tails, and big teeth! Bears are versatile. They can swim, run, stand on two legs, and climb trees. Adult grizzly bears can run up to an incredible 40mph — the same pace as a greyhound. Bears are one of the most intelligent land animals. They have the largest and most complex brains compared to other land mammals their size and are creative and successful in solving problems. Anyone who has tried to secure their campground trash would agree.

Bears represent creativity and adaptability. In life and in business we are thrown many curve balls. We need to tap into our inner bear to unleash our creativity factor.

Walt Disney - Story of Adaptability

Walter Elias Disney co-founded Walt Disney Productions with his brother Roy, which became one of the best-known motion picture production companies in the world.

But the Disney story is one of many pivots, twists, and turns. Walt and Roy's first venture, Laugh-O-Grams, was forced to declare bankruptcy in 1923. The brothers moved to Hollywood and created Walt Disney Studios, but their primary character, Oswald the Lucky Rabbit, was "stolen" by their New York distributor.

But Disney's fortune would change. In 1928, Steamboat Willie, starring Mickey Mouse, opened at a Theater in New York. In 1937,

Disney premiered the first full-length animated film named Snow White and the Seven Dwarfs which won eight Oscars.

In 1955, the Disneyland theme park opened in Anaheim, California. In 1966, Walt died but in 1971, under Roy's leadership Disney World opened in Orlando, Florida. There are 12 Disney theme parks around the world.

Today, Disney is an entertainment conglomerate with over $67 billion in sales. It gets revenue from theme parks, consumer products, media networks, studio entertainment and direct-to-consumer services. Along the way Disney purchased Pixar, Marvel and LucasFilm. Disney still has the magic touch. In 2019, the company introduced a streaming channel named Disney Plus and captured 130 million subscribers in less than two years. And it all began with a mouse.

Thoughts for Reflection

- Be careful if backpacking in Alaska… a person in a sleeping bag might seem like a soft taco to a Kodiak Bear.
- "It's kind of fun to do the impossible." - Walt Disney
- "Laughter is timeless, imagination has no age, dreams are forever."- Walt Disney
- "Creativity is intelligence having fun." - Albert Einstein
- "You can't use up creativity. The more you use, the more you have." - Maya Angelou
- "Bears rose to the top of the food chain solely so they could dedicate half their lives to sleep. It's the world's most intimidating power nap." - James Breakwel
- "Problems are not stop signs; they are guidelines." - Robert H. Schuller
- "We cannot solve problems with the same thinking we used when we created them." - Albert Einstein
- "Oh well, bears will be bears." - Michael Bond
- "Don't wait for the right opportunity. Create it." - George Bernard Shaw
- "The only difference between success and failure is the ability to take action." - Alexander Graham Bell
- "Of all the paths you take in life, make sure a few of them are dirt." - John Muir

- "Change is the constant in life. One's ability to adapt to those changes will determine your success in life." - Benjamin Franklin
- "Action and adaptability create opportunity." - Garrison Wynn
- "Adaptability is being able to adjust to any situation at any given time." - John Wooden
- "Start where you are. Use what you have. Do what you can." - Arthur Ashe
- "Creative isn't the way I think, it's the way I like to live." - Paul Sandip
- "To coexist, people need to 'understand bears', the bear is intelligent and resourceful….Fear is not necessary. Understanding, compassion, and tolerance is." - Mike McIntosh
- "The best way of being kind to bears is not to be very close to them." - Margaret Atwood
- "Bears not only make the habitat rich, they enrich us just by being." - Linda Jo Hunter

Chapter 14: Crocodile

"An appeaser is one who feeds a crocodile,
hoping it will eat him last."
- Winston Churchill

Chapter 14: Crocodile - The Ambusher

Crocodiles are large, predatory, reptiles with sharp teeth and have the strongest bite of any animal in the world. They swim well and are fast on land at short distances. Most are solitary and territorial; they utilize a stalk and ambush prey hunting strategy. We cannot underestimate the cunning nor the intelligence of these creatures.

Crocodiles are ambush hunters that utilize a variety of strategies in hunting behavior. They quietly and patiently wait in watering holes for animals to take a drink. The thirsty and unsuspecting animal is surprised when an animal with massive teeth and jaws leaps out at them and drags them into the water. A few crocodilian species use sticks and branches to lure nest-building birds. They will balance twigs on their snouts and lie very still. When the bird tries to perch or grab the sticks, the croc will lunge and grab the bird.

Moreover, some have been observed hunting their prey collaboratively and cooperatively. Renowned nineteenth century Biologist Nicholas Miklouho-Maclay watched "collaborative fishing" at work. At times a croc would swim in a circle around a shoal of fish. The fish would be forced into a tight ball. The other crocodiles would take turns snatching fish by cutting across the center of the ball. Or a larger crocodile would chase fish towards shallow water by splashing its large and powerful tail, where smaller more agile crocs would be waiting to feast.

Crocodiles are symbolic of the threats that take us by surprise. We might be ambushed by a health crisis, loss of a partner, employment, or a big client. Sometimes we have prior warning and other times we are taken completely by surprise. Whatever the event, it can be devastating. It can throw our entire world into chaos.

D-Day

On June 6, 1944, 'D-Day', allied forces launched the largest amphibious invasion in the history of warfare. The combined forces of the United States, British, and Canadian military installations stormed five beachheads in Normandy, France. The Allied landings marked the start of a long and costly campaign to liberate Northwest Europe from Nazi occupation and end the Second World War.

Prior to D-Day, the Allies conducted a large-scale deception campaign designed to mislead the Germans about the intended invasion target. They utilized double agents, fake radio transmissions and a "phantom army" to trick the Nazis into thinking they would invade Pas-de-Calais. They focused on surprising the enemy.

My friend David Henderson notes that the Marines are the crocodiles of the US armed services. The Marine Corp is its own branch but falls under the administration of the U. S. Department of the Navy. Its sister service is the U.S. Navy. They are an offensive amphibious assault machine and some of their Naval vessels are even called "Gator ships". Death Before Dishonor is the Marine theme. Semper Fidelis - Always faithful to God, Country, Corps and Family.

Application

We get ambushed by crocodiles in other ways. Our car breaks down and we need to repair it. We hope that we can cover the unplanned repair costs.

We discover that our roof is leaking, there are termites or black mold growing somewhere. Once again, we have been ambushed.

There is perhaps no bigger crocodile than a health crisis. Having a heart attack, stroke or learning you have cancer puts us face to face with our mortality. Having a loved one die or be in a life-threatening accident can be equally challenging. One's medical status or health can change in an instant. You can get ambushed by a medical emergency. People suddenly discover the harsh reality that health insurance does not cover everything. A catastrophic illness can be devastating physically, mentally, and financially. In 2019 over 137 million Americans faced financial hardship due to medical debt.

Thoughts for Reflection

- "I don't care who the biggest fish in the pond is. I'm a whole different animal (crocodile)." - Unknown

- "Accidents ambush the unsuspecting, often violently, just like love." - Andrew Davidson

- "How cheerfully he seems to grin, how neatly spreads his claws, and welcomes little fishes in, with gently smiling jaws." - Lewis Carroll

- "Don't think there are no crocodiles because the water is calm." - Malaysian Proverb

- "Love is a crocodile just above the water line waiting to attack the innocent herbivore of my freedom." - Dov Davidoff

- Even a thirsty man will not drink at the river where a crocodile waits." - Timothy G. Bax

- "Like the crocodile, he always strikes at the weakest spot." - George Orwell

- "The crocodile doesn't harm the bird that cleans his teeth for him. He eats the others but not that one." - Linda Hogan

- “Not all storms come to disrupt your life, some come to clear our path.” - Anonymous

- “I suppose it’s like the ticking crocodile, isn’t it? Time is chasing after all of us.”- J.M. Barrie

- “To expect the unexpected shows a thoroughly modern intellect.” - Oscar Wilde

- “Resilience is all about being able to overcome the unexpected. Sustainability is about survival. The goal of resilience is to thrive.” - Jamais Cascio

- “Sometimes life takes you on unexpected paths, and those paths aren't always in the same direction.” - Jonathan Scott

- “The only real things in life are the unexpected things. Everything else is just an illusion.” - Watkin Tudor Jones

- “The truth is you don't know what is going to happen tomorrow. Life is a crazy ride, and nothing is guaranteed.” - Eminem

Final Thoughts for Reflection

- "Let us endeavor to live so that when we come to die even the undertaker will be sorry." - Mark Twain

- "Life's too short to wake up with regrets. So, love the people who treat you right, forgive the ones that don't believe everything happens for a reason. If you get a chance, take it. If it changes your life, let it. Nobody said it'd be easy, they just promised it would be worth it." - Dr. Seuss

- "Life is the only art that we are required to practice without preparation, and without being allowed the preliminary trials, the failures and botches, that are essential for training." - Lewis Mumford

- "Say you were standing with one foot in the oven and one foot in an ice bucket. According to the percentage of people, you would be perfectly comfortable." - Bobby Bragan

- "Never lose hope...Storms make people stronger and never last forever." - Roy T. Bennett

- "It is better to be divided by the truth than to be united in error." - Adrian Rogers

- "Life isn't about finding yourself. Life is about creating yourself." - George Bernard Shaw

- “The purpose of life, after all, is to live it, to taste experience to the utmost, to reach out eagerly and without fear for newer and richer experience.” - Eleanor Roosevelt
- “Life is really simple, but we insist on making it complicated.” - Confucius
- “Nothing in life is to be feared, it is only to be understood. Now is the time to understand more, so that we may fear less.” - Marie Curie
- “Do not dwell in the past, do not dream of the future, concentrate the mind on the present moment.” - Buddha
- “We do not remember days, we remember moments.” - Cesare Pavese
- “Babies are such a nice way to start people.” - Don Herold
- “It takes considerable knowledge just to realize the extent of your own ignorance.” - Thomas Sowell
- “Now this is not the end. It is not even the beginning of the end. But it is, perhaps, the end of the beginning.” - Winston Churchill
- “**Vulnerability** is hard and it’s **scary** and it **feels dangerous**. But it’s not as hard, or **scary** or **dangerous** as getting to the end of our lives and having to ask ourselves: What if I would’ve **shown up**?” - Brene Brown

- “What you have become is the price you paid to get what you used to want.” - Mignon McLaughlin
- “I learned long ago, never to wrestle with a pig. You get dirty, and besides, the pig likes it.” - George Bernard Shaw
- “If you can find a path with no obstacles, it probably doesn’t lead anywhere.” - Frank A. Clark
- “Focus on where you want to go, not on what you fear.”- Tony Robbins
- “In business or in life, don’t follow the wagon tracks too closely.” - H. Jackson Brown, Jr.
- How old would you be if you didn’t know how old you were?” - Leroy “Satchel” Paige
- “Some men never find the key to success because they don’t look in the right place - inside their own minds.” - B.C. Forbes
- “The purpose of life, after all, is to live it, to taste experience to the utmost, to reach out eagerly and without fear for newer and richer experiences.” - Eleanor Roosevelt
- “The very least you can do in your life is figure out what you hope for. And the most you can do is live inside that hope. Not admire it from a distance but live right in it, under its roof.” - Barbara Kingsolver
- Make your bed every morning and never go to bed at night with dirty dishes in the sink...as this helps build character in our lives.
- “Things ain’t what they used to be and never were.” - Will Rogers

- “If there is a book that you want to read, but it hasn’t been written yet, then you must write it.” - Toni Morrison
- “Remember not only to say the right thing in the right place, but to leave unsaid the wrong thing at the tempting moment.” - Benjamin Franklin
- “Press on. Nothing can take the place of persistence. Talent will not; nothing is more common than unsuccessful men with talent. Genius will not; the world is full of educated derelicts. **Perseverance and determination alone are omnipotent**.” - Calvin Coolidge
- “Our lives begin to end the day we become silent about things that matter.” - Martin Luther King Jr.
- “I tend to live in the past because most of my life is there.” - Herb Caen
- “Always do right. It will please some people and astonish the rest.” - Mark Twain
- “If you don’t look facts in the face, they have a way of stabbing you in the back.” - Winston Churchill
- “Children have never been very good at listening to their elders, but they have never failed to imitate them.” - James Baldwin
- “Live in such a way that you would not be ashamed to sell your parrot to the town gossip.” - Will Rogers
- “Be yourself; everyone else is already taken.” - Oscar Wilde
- “In order that people may be happy in their work, these three things are needed: They must be fit for it. They must

not do too much of it. And they must have a sense of success in it." - John Ruskin

- "Faith is taking the first step even when you don't see the whole staircase." - Martin Luther King Jr.
- "The men who try to do something and fail are infinitely better than those who try to do nothing and succeed." - Lloyd Jones
- "Your rewards in life are always in direct proportion to your contribution - your service." - Earl Nightingale
- Try to live on the principle – "Nothing attempted, nothing gained and is resolved that if he fails, he is going to fail while trying to succeed." - Wilfred Peterson
- "There are powers inside of you which, if you could discover and use, would make of you everything you ever dreamed or imagined you could become." - Orison Sweet Marden
- "The things you do for yourself are gone when you are gone, but the things you do for others remain as your legacy." - Kalu Ndukwe Kalu
- "It's amazing how little tomorrow can make up for a whole lot of yesterday." - John Guare
- "It's never too late to be what we might have been." - George Eliot
- "You should worry less about who you might offend and care more about who you might inspire." – Tim Allen

- "Children are the living messages we send to a time we will not see." - Neil Postman
- When flatterers meet, the devil goes to dinner." English proverb
- "When lending people money, be sure their character exceeds their collateral." - H. Jackson Brown, Jr.
- "Never buy a Rolex from someone who's out of breath." - Unknown
- "I can explain to you, but I can't comprehend it for you." - Edward I. Koch
- Without goals...we find ourselves in a rut...and a rut is like a grave with the ends knocked out. - Earl Nightingale
- "Be brave enough to live the life of your dreams according to your vision and purpose instead of the expectations and opinions of others." - Roy T. Bennett
- "Mistakes are always forgivable, if one has the courage to admit them." - Bruce Lee
- "Your reputation is what others think of you: your character is what you truly are." - Bohdi Sanders
- "It's not the things that we get but the hearts that we touch that will determine our success in life." - Mac Anderson
- "Measure your wealth not by the things you have but by the things for which you would not take money." - Dave Ramsey
- "Laughter is the shortest distance between two people." - Victor Borge

- "Ask someone you'd like to know better to list 5 people they would most like to meet. It will tell you a lot about him." - H. Jackson Brown
- "Three things you cannot recover in life: the WORD after it's said, the MOMENT after it's missed, and the TIME after it's gone." - Ziad K. Abdelnour
- "I don't make jokes. I just watch the government and report the facts." - Will Rogers
- "If one advances confidently in the direction of his dreams, and endeavors to live the life which he has imagined, he will meet with a success unexpected in common hours." - Henry David Thoreau
- For clarity of life, we should...
  "Plan with attitude,
  prepare with aptitude,
  participate with servitude,
  receive with gratitude,
  and that should be enough to separate you from the multitudes." - Krish Dhanam

Self-Assessment

1. What animal do you think you are most like?
2. Why do you think you are this animal?
3. What are some positive/negative qualities that your animal has that can relate to you?
4. What animal do you want to be?
5. What animal would your best friend guess that you are?
6. What animal are you most different from?
7. Does it surprise you that you are this animal?
8. What animal would your best friend or significant other be?
9. What is the second animal that you are most like?
10. If someone were to guess your animal, would they get it right?
11. What animal has the scariest characteristics?
12. What animal has the sweetest characteristics?
13. How do you rate success?
14. How do you rate failure?
15. What is the number one quality that you have to share with others?
16. "The 3 C's of Life: Choices, Chances, Changes. You must make a choice to take a chance, or your life will never change." - Zig Ziglar

    Which one of the three will it be?

The Back Nine...and Then it's Winter

Time has a way of moving quickly and catching us unaware of the passing years. It seems like yesterday that I was young, just married and embarking on our new life. It seems like so long ago. I wonder where all the years went. I know that I lived them all. I have glimpses of how it was back then and of all my hopes and dreams.

But suddenly here it is. I am in the "back nine" of my life and it catches me by surprise. How did it get here so fast? Where did the years go and where did my youth go?

I remember seeing older people through the years and thinking that those older people were years away from me. I was only "on the first hole" and "the back nine" was so far off that I could not imagine what it would be like.

I used to tell those younger than me, "I was what you are, you will be what I am." The original quote by Horace was in Latin, "Eram quod es, eris quod sum."

But here it is, my friends are now gray and retired. They move slower and I see myself as an older person now. Some are in better shape than me and a few are in worse shape than me. I see the great change, not like the ones I remember who were young and vibrant. But, like me, their age is beginning to show, and we are now those older folks that we used to see and never thought we'd become.

So now we enter this new season of life unprepared for all the aches and pains and the loss of strength and ability to go and do things that we wish we had done but never did! At least we know that we're on the "back nine". We're not sure how long it will last. We know that when it's over on this earth, it's over. A new adventure will begin! There are things we wish we hadn't done, things we should have done, but indeed, there are many things we're happy to have done. It's all in a lifetime.

So, if you're not on the "back nine" yet, let me remind you, that it will be here faster than you think. So, whatever you would like to accomplish in your life please do it quickly! Don't put things off too long! Life goes by very fast. Do what you can today, as you can never be sure whether you're on the "back nine" or not!

You have no promise that you will see all the seasons of your life. Live for today and say all the things that you want your loved ones to remember. I hope that they appreciate and love you for all the things that you have meant for them in all the years past!

Life is a gift to you. The way you live your life is your gift to those who come after you. Make it a fantastic one. Live it well! Enjoy today! Do something fun! Be happy! Have a great life!

- "It is health that is real wealth and not pieces of gold and silver."- Mahatma Gandhi

Lastly, remember this, your kids are becoming you, but your grandchildren are perfect! Going out is good, but coming home is better! You forget names, but it's okay because other people forgot they even knew you! The things you used to care to do, you no longer care to do, but you really do care that you don't care to do them anymore. You miss the days when everything worked with just an "ON" and "OFF" switch. You tend to use more 4 letter words such as what and when. Now that you can afford expensive jewelry, it's not safe to wear it anywhere. You notice everything they sell in stores are sleeveless! What used to be freckles are now liver spots. Everybody whispers. You have 3 sizes of clothes in your closet, 2 sizes of which you will never wear. But old is good in some things: old songs, old movies, and the best of all old friends and acquaintances. Stay well.

- "It is not what you gather but what you scatter that tells what kind of life you have lived." - Helen Walton

- "Today is the oldest you've ever been, and the youngest you'll ever be again." - Eleanor Roosevelt

So, enjoy each day while it lasts. Clock builders of the world build the foundation upon which success begins to grow...time tellers however never get the roof on until after the rain begins.

Made in the USA
Columbia, SC
21 July 2022

63778110R00061